Thanksgiving Day

Cadie Buckholdt

Rigby®
A Harcourt Achieve Imprint

www.Rigby.com
1-800-531-5015

Long ago, the Pilgrims came to live
in a new land.
They came a long way on a
small ship.

The Pilgrims sailed all the way from
Europe to North America!
It took a long time.

The Pilgrims made houses to live in. They used wood and grass to build their houses.

They learned to grow their own
food, too.

Native Americans helped the
Pilgrims in their new land.

The Pilgrims had a big feast.
They invited Native Americans to
join them.

They were thankful for their food.
It was the first Thanksgiving.

Many people today still have a feast
on Thanksgiving Day.
They say thank you for the things
they have.

A feast is just one thing to do
on Thanksgiving Day.
There are other things to do, too.

Thanksgiving is also a big day
for football.
Many people watch a game.

Some people put out things for the Thanksgiving holiday.

Other people go to a
Thanksgiving parade.
The parades can have big balloons,
bands, and clowns.

People stand on the side of the
street to watch the parade.
They smile as the parade goes by.

Some people help others on Thanksgiving Day.

They give food to people who
don't have much to eat.

Every Thanksgiving, people do
many things.
What do you do for Thanksgiving Day?